Meditations
on
the Lord's Prayer

Meditations
on
the Lord's Prayer

Pastor Michael L. Faber

Elk Grove Publications

Elk Grove, CA

ISBN-13: 978-1-940781-00-6

Elk Grove Publications
9124 Elk Grove Blvd.
Elk Grove, CA 95624
United States of America

Printed in United States of America

THE LORD'S PRAYER

Matthew 6:9-13

(King James Version-KJV)

Our Father, which art in heaven, Hallowed be thy name.

Thy kingdom come, Thy will be done in earth, as it is in heaven.

Give us this day our daily bread.

And forgive us our debts, as we forgive our debtors.

And lead us not into temptation, but deliver us from evil:

For thine is the kingdom, and the power, and the glory, forever. Amen.

INTRODUCTION

When we were little children being taught to pray at our bedside, often the first prayer we learned was *The Lord's Prayer*. Every Sunday, in many congregations, in many denominations, across the world, Christians of every size and stripe recite *The Lord's Prayer*. We see this prayer on plaques hanging in devout homes, as well as on the side of coffee cups.

Christians have had *The Lord's Prayer* ever since Jesus was preaching the Sermon on the Mount and someone asked him *Lord teach us to pray*. *The Lord's Prayer* appears twice in the Bible. First at Matthew 6:9-13 in the context of the Sermon on the Mount and also at Luke 11:2-4 where an abbreviated version of the Lord's Prayer is recorded.

The Church has loved Matthew's version the best, and this prayer has been in use since the earliest days of Christendom. Some of the earliest post biblical church documents encourage individual Christians to pray *The Lord's Prayer* three times a day. Churches began incorporating *The Lord's Prayer* into their liturgy from the earliest time as well.

Well, when should we use *The Lord's Prayer* and how should it be used? This is an individual choice. Certainly, we should teach it to small children for their memorization. It is also properly used in church during the liturgy, and in groups, when communal prayer out loud is a good idea.

There have been times of stress and emergency in many lives over the years where people hold hands and recite *The Lord's Prayer* together during great turmoil. This can be a powerful time of unity and comfort. I do not advocate

2

RESTRICTING one's prayers to *The Lord's Prayer* or any other kind of pre-composed prayer. I am no fan of reciting rote prayers without thinking, meaning or intent. I believe prayer must be from the heart of the Believer to God, but that said, we certainly can be free to pray the exact words of *The Lord's Prayer* if we mean them and think about them, or to use His prayer as a model for our own individual prayers. We can use the psalms in a like fashion.

During the Middle Ages, Teresa of Avila, taught that prayer must be a contemplation of God, and a time of growing closer to God. Rather than the mere recitation of words, she taught her sisters to meditate on each line of *The Lord's Prayer* in an effort to keep God in mind and to stay in the presence of God. Each line would reveal a different attribute of God. She suggested that they take an entire hour to work their way through *The Lord's Prayer* once. She wrote a detailed commentary on *The Lord's Prayer*.

This little book takes a similar approach.

Below are six sermons that I have preached. Each sermon focuses on one line of *The Lord's Prayer*, delving into the mysteries of that line as revealed to me at the time of my sermon preparation.

I invite you to join me on a journey through *The Lord's Prayer*, to look at each line in depth and think about what Jesus was revealing to us in this short little prayer. Then in your own time, after you have read this booklet, spend time with the Lord yourself and pray *The Lord's Prayer* slowly, as taught by Teresa of Avila, and think about the mysteries of God.

Meditate on his graciousness, his holiness, his forgiveness. Ask God how you should react to these things in your own life, as you work through *The Lord's Prayer* line by line. Enjoy.

OUR FATHER WHO ART IN HEAVEN

How Is God the Father?

In one way, as Creator, God is the Father of us all, since He created us and gave us life. As Creator, He programmed us, formed us, and made us the way we are. He established how we react to various stimuli. He determined what makes us succeed and what makes us fail. As He created the Universe, He also set up the rules and divvies out the rewards and the punishments. He decides what is good, and gives rewards, and He decides what is bad, and metes out punishment for such behavior.

Many ancient religions, especially the Jews and the Muslims, understand this about God, and for them, there is a very direct relationship in behavior between reward and punishment. They are taught to fear God and to respect His rules and laws, lest punishment swiftly be forthcoming.

This is okay, for the beginning of our relationship with God, for as the Old Testament itself proclaims, *The fear of the Lord is the beginning of knowledge. Proverbs 1:7.*

Every small child must fear the rod or the discipline of his or her parent, so that they will learn the necessary skills of survival before they understand the whys and wherefores of the dangers of this world. The small child knows to fear the punishment of daddy if they play with power tools or cross busy streets, even if they don't understand the nature of the danger itself.

Jesus Brought Us to A New Understanding

When Jesus Christ walked this earth, He taught His followers a new understanding of the Almighty Lord God of Hosts. Jehovah God was more than just Creator and fearsome Judge of righteousness and wickedness. He was also Father. He, according to Jesus, was a loving Father, who loved us so much that He sent His only Son in the flesh, to die for us, so that we could become part of His forever family.

In His most beloved parable of the *Prodigal Son*, Jesus taught us of the loving and patient nature of Father God. He is the Father who waits and pines for our return to His loving embrace.

In the Lord's Prayer, He teaches us to address the Almighty Creator of the Universe with the words, *Our Father.*

This is amazing, knowing what we do about Christ. We understand that Christ is the Second Person of the Trinity, which consists of God the Father, God the Son and God the Holy Spirit. Amazingly, He does not pray, *My Father*, but instead teaches us to pray, *Our Father.*

We understand that Father God is the loving Father of the Son, but by these words, Christ is including us in *His* Family. And this is how it should be. You have heard that *God is love.* This love consisted from before all time in the loving relationship between the Father, the Son and the Holy Spirit. This love was so great, that the Father decided not to contain it, but allow it to spill out, which resulted in the creation of the Universe.

I saw something on Face Book which stated that "All we are is recycled Star Dust." From an evolutionary viewpoint, we can agree, that our bodies might be created from star dust, but what about our spirits? And from where did the star dust come, but from the overflowing love of God?

I say, "We are the recycled love of God which He did not contain." God allowed His love to spill forth into the Creation because He wanted to expand His circle of love to include Creation, which means you and me.

Jesus came to share this. To reconcile us to God the Father so that we cannot just be His Creation, and subject to His rule, but to be His Children and embraced by His love!

But how is it possible that we can dare approach the Creator God in the way Jesus suggests? How can we become part of God's forever family? How do we move from mere creation, to beloved son or daughter?

Paul states in the book of Romans, *But, if Christ is in you, your body is dead because of sin, yet your spirit is alive because of righteousness. And if the Spirit of Him who raised Jesus from the dead is living in you, He who raised Christ from the dead will also give life to your mortal bodies through his Spirit who lives in you. Romans 8:12-13.*

In other words, by receiving Christ as Lord and Savior, we actually receive the Spirit of God, who LIVES IN US! This Spirit of God now dwelling within, gives us not just legal right to claim God as Father, like in adoption, but actually gives us familial commonality with the Father, through the Son.

Stated another way, when we receive Christ as Savior and Lord, the Spirit of the Lord enters us and gives us HOLY SPIRIT DNA, so that we are no longer merely creations of God, but His children as well!

Paul declares, *The Spirit himself, testifies with our spirit, that we are God's children. Romans 8:16.* Knowing that God is Father and we are His children, what does this say about who He is and who we are?

What Does God Do as Father?

What does any father do? He provides, He protects, and He punishes. He makes sure there is food on the table. He keeps his kids safe from harm, and He does the best he can to instill through rewards and punishments, a sense of values and discipline in his children so that when they go forward in life, things will go well for them.

In the Lord's Prayer we see all three of these functions at work, or at least implicated.

PROVISION:

In the Lord's Prayer we ask *our Father to give us our daily bread.* We are asking God to provide for our daily needs, which is something He desires to do.

PROTECTION:

In the Lord's Prayer, we pray, *Lead us not into temptation, but deliver us from the evil one.* We are praying for the Father to protect us and keep us from harm both, physical and spiritual. Again this is something that He desires to do. Every loving parent desires to keep their children from harm.

PUNISHMENT:

In the Lord's Prayer, we ask God to forgive our debts as we forgive our debtors. In essence, we are seeking to avoid some of the punishment we deserve, by means of forgiveness, IF we are willing to share that forgiveness with others.

Elsewhere, in the Bible we are informed that we will be punished in this life for sins committed, so in essence, what we are really seeking by this prayer is mitigation of temporal punishment, as well as reconciliation with God, and forgiveness in the eternal realm. In the book of Hebrews, the writer states, *Endure hardship as discipline; God is treating you as sons… God disciplines us for our own good, that we may share in his holiness No discipline seems pleasant at the time, but painful. Later on, however, it produces a harvest of righteousness and peace for those who have been trained by it." Hebrews 12:7, 10-11.*

If we are God's children, He will discipline us, maybe even more than He disciplines His creation.

I know that as a child of God, I never get away with anything! Others can persist in crime and sin, seemingly impervious to the consequences, but me? I get caught every time, almost immediately. That is due to the discipline of the Father. He doesn't want me walking that path, and He ensures I have every chance to get off the road of wickedness as soon as possible!

I remember when I was about fourteen years old, my friend and I decided we were going to steal something from a Hippie Health Food store. We justified this because we didn't like hippies. We went into the store. The plan was that my friend would distract the clerk, while I snatched something and walked out of the store.

The plan worked perfectly. He distracted the clerk, and I casually picked up a health food bar and put it in my jacket pocket and exited the store. He soon followed. As we were walking down the street, I was subconsciously unwrapping the health food bar and thinking, "My, that was easy, and even exciting. Instead of the Hippie store, maybe we could go up the road to the Mall and I could go into the Pharmacy and steal something good, like stamps or marbles, instead of this stupid health food bar."

As I was planning my next caper, I lifted the bar to my mouth to take a bite, and my friend cried out, "EWWWW!" I looked at the bar and it was full of maggots! Even at this young age, I immediately looked to heaven and prayed, "Thank you God! I get it!"

God was punishing me, and by this swift and direct punishment, He kept me from walking the path of thievery. I never shoplifted again. As Father, God punishes.

What Should We Do As Children?

As children of God, our responsibility is to love, obey and belong.

Love the Father

As children of God, who love our Father, we should seek His company often, speak to him, share our burdens and concerns, ask Him for what we desire, and also ask Him how we can help him.

All of you know this is true, especially if you are older teens or young adults. If you love your parents, the best way you can show your love is by BEING WITH THEM. Visit them, call them. Stop by and talk to them. They really want very little else from you other than you being the best you, you can be.

On the other hand if you don't love your parents, you likely would want to avoid them and spend as little time as possible in their presence. When I was a teenager, I heard a sermon by Juan Carlos Ortiz. It affected my view on this subject. He set forth the following skit:

Monday Morning, I am eating breakfast and reading the newspaper. The Lord Jesus is at my breakfast table trying to get my attention, waving his arms and trying to make eye contact, but I just look away or look right though him. I don't acknowledge His presence.

Monday afternoon, as I am working and talking and going about my daily chores, the Lord Jesus is jumping up and down. As I proceed with my routine., I am entirely ignoring Him.

Monday night, I eat my dinner and watch a movie which is clearly grieving Jesus, but I don't care and I don't see Him despite his repeated attempts to catch my attention.

At bedtime, I say, "*Good night Lord.*" Jesus says, "*Good Night, my child.*" And I immediately fall asleep.

Tuesday Morning, afternoon and night, I go through the same routine, and except a quick good night at bed time, I entirely ignore the Lord. The same is true for Wednesday, Thursday, Friday, and Saturday.

Then something changes on Sunday. I wake up in the morning, put on my best clothes, and Jesus is watching. I get into the car and He sits next to me. Finally, I get to church and I look over and see Jesus with me, and I cry out, "*Praise the Lord, Hallelujah!*" I begin kissing the Lord, dancing with

Him, and hugging Him, while proclaiming, "*I love you, I love you.*" The Lord is flabbergasted, but eats up the attention, and then when an hour passes, I leave the church, and go back to my routine of entirely ignoring the Lord through the rest of the week!

This is a sad but funny example of what many of us really do in our Christian lives. If we really loved God, however, would we really want to ignore Him all week long, only to give Him attention one hour a week? No, if we love God as His children, we should want to BE WITH HIM as much as possible.

We should spend time throughout the week singing praises, reading His word, thinking about Him and talking with Him. This is the best way to show our love. What else should we do as His children?

Obey The Father

As children, not only should we LOVE the Father, but we also need to OBEY the Father.

When we were 5 years old, we were taught through rewards and punishment to obey our parents. If you did not obey, you knew that a spanking or time on the wall, or some other disciplinary action was soon coming. So we obeyed, because we feared.

As we matured into teens and young adults, we continued to obey our parents not only because we feared punishment, but because we realized that Dad and Mom knew more about the world than we did. We obeyed them because we respected them. Likewise, we obeyed because we did not want to defy and rebel against our parents; we did not want to dishonor them. We obeyed out of love.

Likewise, we should obey God, not just out of fear of punishment, but also out of respect and love. Paul said that the spirit of fear had been removed and replaced with a spirit of son-ship. As sons, we obey as sons, out of love and respect for the Father.

Belong to the Father

Paul said, *Now, if we are children, then we are heirs—heirs of God and co-heirs with Christ, IF INDEED we share in his sufferings in order that we may share in his glory." Romans 8:17 [NIV-Emphasis added].*

Children are typically heirs to the estate of the parents. If the parents are wealthy, they will be wealthy. If the parents lose all their money in a bad investment the children likewise lose. If the reputations of the parents are high, the children reap the benefits by associating with all kinds of important and famous people.

Likewise if the reputation of the father is bad, the children may suffer as well. As children, our fortunes are tied to that of our father.

As this is true, spiritually as well as naturally, we desire the success of our Father in the cosmic battle of good versus evil. If the Father is winning, then we enjoy the esteem of the community if we are good Christians. But, if He is losing, the community may despise us.

14

As God's children our fates are tied to His. The same is true for the local church to which we belong. If our Church is known for its good works in the community, we gain something by association with the church. But, if our church is known for a scandal, we are all ashamed.

Since we, who believe, are all children of the same Father, we are all brothers and sisters in Christ, and belong to the same forever- family. We are in this together not only with God, but with each other!

As co-heirs with Jesus, we are also tied to His fate. We know He has risen from the dead and will sit with His Father in glory, and we will be with Him. But if we want to share in this glory, we must first join Him in His suffering.

Notice that in the Scripture above, our enjoyment as the status of co-heir is conditional on our willingness to share in His sufferings! Paul says we are co-heirs IF INDEED we share in Christ's sufferings in order to share in his glory.

We all know what a *fair weather friend* is. It is a person who only comes around when times are good for you and they want to share your joy and your money, but as soon as life gets hard or difficulties arise, they disappear. True friends stand together in thick and thin.

To be a co-heir with Jesus, we need to stand with Him in thick and thin. Yes, we will enjoy glory someday, but in this life and in this world, we can often expect opposition, harassment, and even persecution if we try to follow the path of Christ.

In some countries such as Muslim and Communist countries, pastors are beaten, or imprisoned or killed, or their property destroyed just because they proclaim Christ. These are true martyrs. But even in relatively free countries such as the U.S. or Europe, you will suffer with Christ as well if you are faithful. How so?

U.S. military officers are told not to share their faith with their subordinates, boy scout organizations are cut off from public funding, individual Christians are ridiculed or scorned, teachers are not hired, scientists are excluded, all because they hold true to their convictions instead of going along with the crowd.

As a teenager, you may suffer for acting as you know you should, instead of going along with your friends and doing something stupid. If you regularly choose Jesus, you may find yourself socially ostracized. You may suffer quietly by following Jesus, just for telling the truth instead of lying on applications for jobs, credit, or public assistance...

But, I believe that every time you suffer for being honest and true, and hold to your faith, God will make it up to you in some other way. Indeed, in our Scripture, we know that by being willing to suffer with Christ now, guarantees our status as co-heirs. Just as our Co-heir faced the cross then, we face the cross, now. But, just as He will be glorified, so shall we.

We have seen, so far, that Christ has taught us to pray, *Our Father* to indicate that we are children of God, and not just a creation. We have seen, that by placing our faith in Christ, we receive the Holy Spirit, making us not only legally adopted children but giving us Holy Spirit DNA!

We have seen that as a Father, God *Provides, Protects and Punishes* us, and that as a Child of God, we *Love, Obey and Belong* to the Father. Knowing all of this, how should being a Child of God, as opposed to a mere creation of God, affect our prayer?

Attitude of Prayer

When we pray, now, we can approach God as a close one who loves us, rather than a fearsome far off entity. God is close to us. He cares. If you were to approach a King or a powerful Emperor with a petition, you would first have to establish

1) Who you are, and–

2) Why he should care about your petition.

With God as our Father, we are not approaching some far off sovereign, but our Dad who loves us and wants nothing but good for us.

Paul said that through Christ Jesus we trade a spirit of slavery to fear with a spirit of Son-ship, and that through the spirit, we cry "Abba, Father".

Abba means daddy. How would a slave approach a fearsome Master with a personal request?

How would a 10 year old daughter approach her daddy with the same request?

The first would approach with fear, the second with confidence.

As we pray, we should pray as children beloved by the Father, with the confidence that our Father loves us and desires our good.

Perhaps the slave and the daughter will each receive a "no", but each will approach with a different attitude, and the answer may be given for different reasons.

The Master may tell the slave, "No" because the Master does not want to be bothered, or he may not feel that the slave is deserving of the request.

The Father will only tell the daughter, "No" if her request is not good for her. Otherwise, He is pleased that she approached and is always looking for good to bless her with.

Sometimes good parents must tell their children, "No." for their own good, no matter how much they scream and cry.

In Kentucky, a 5 year old just killed his 2 year old sister after receiving a pellet gun that he desired. A 5 year old has no business with a gun, and the parents who were pleased to grant the 5 year old his heart's desire did not exercise good judgment. This led to tragic consequences.

Fortunately, our Father in heaven loves to please us, but also exercises good judgment. Through Jesus, we can *approach the throne of Grace with a sincere heart full of assurance of faith, having our hearts sprinkled to cleanse us from a guilty conscience…Hebrews 10:22.*

Call

What can we make of this? God indeed created each of us, and He has established rules for us to live by or face the consequences. But He desires that we will be more than just obedient or disobedient creations subject to His judgment and wrath. He also desires to adopt us into His forever-family through His Son Jesus Christ.

He wants our love and belonging as well as our obedience. If we will put our faith in Jesus, we will receive into us the same Holy Spirit that raised Christ from the dead. We will receive that Holy Spirit DNA!

God created us to love us. Will we love Him back? Will we become part of His forever family?

Reflections:

OUR FATHER WHO ART IN HEAVEN

1. How do you primarily see God?

2. As an angry judge or a loving Father? Someone who doesn't care about your life or as someone who watches everything you do? Something else?

3. How did you interact with your own father? Did that relationship have any bearing on what kind of Father you envision God?

4. How should parents discipline their children?

5. In what manner does God discipline you? Why does He do this?

6. In what ways do you show love to God as Father? Do you spend time with Him? How much, how often? Is this enough? If not, what could you do to change this?

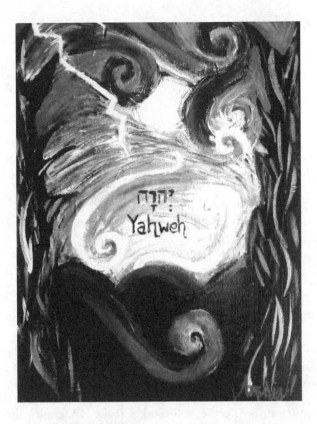

HALLOWED BE THY NAME

THERE IS POWER IN THE NAME OF THE LORD

Matt: 6:9This then is how you should pray:
'Our Father who art in heaven,
Hallowed be thy name...'

Introduction

Many Christians repeat the Lord's Prayer; *Our Father who art in heaven, hallowed be thy Name...* and wonder just what does *hallowed be thy Name* even mean?

Truth is, many Americans do not even know what *hallowed* means. It is Old English for the word, *holy*. Okay, we start again. *Our Father in heaven, holy is your Name...*

Why are we praying to God, telling Him his Name is holy? Doesn't He already know that? What is worse, when we examine the Greek word used for *hallowed*, it is agiosthetw– which is really a *command* and not just a *description*.

Therefore, instead of telling God that His Name is holy, we are commanding Him to make His Name holy, in kind of a passive way like, "Let your Name be made holy."

Why do we need to tell God to make His name holy? I asked my seminary professor, Rev. Peter Rodgers, who knows more Greek than I do, and he opined that 'The imperative here probably indicates that we pray that the reality (God's name is and has always been holy) may become a reality in the individual or church praying the prayer.'

I'm not sure if he is right, but it makes sense. We are not telling God to make His name holy for its own sake, because it already is holy, but we are asking God, instead to make the holiness of His Name a reality in our own life, and the life of our church.

As in the Third Commandment, set forth in Exodus 20:7(NIV), *You shall not misuse the Name of the LORD your God, for the LORD will not hold anyone guiltless who misuses his name.*

In the King James Version, it reads, *Thou shalt not use the Lord's name in vain.* The Hebrew word for *misuse or vain*, is pronounced SHVA, and it literally means to make empty or worthless.

These two verses, Matt. 6:9 and Exodus 20:7 are like flip sides of the same coin. In the Ten Commandments, God says, *Don't make my Name worthless* and in Matt. 6:9, Jesus teaches us to ask God to make His Name Holy for us.

What makes God's Name Holy, and what does it mean to make His Name worthless? Why is this even important to us as Christians?

What's In A Name?

How many of you even know what God's Name is? Most people don't, because in many English Translations of the Bible, it rarely appears, even though it is written out 5200 times in the Hebrew Old Testament!

The King James Version writes God's Name out as Jehovah. In modern English, you might see it spelled as Yahweh, which is a little closer to the Hebrew lettering, although it really should be Yahveh.

In Ancient Hebrew, the language of the Old Testament, the Name of God is written out as four letters. YHWH, with no vowels. This is the Name that appears over and over again, But, most of the time, in English bibles, you will not see Jehovah or Yahweh spelled out, but rather the word LORD, in all capital letters. What's that all about?

The Old Testament makes it clear that we should not misuse the Name of the Lord, and that God would not hold anyone who did so guiltless. This scared the Ancient Israelites to such a degree, that they refuse to literally pronounce the Name of God. When they are reading the Old Testament and come across the letters YHWH, rather than pronouncing the name, they will substitute the word, *Adonai,* instead.

Adonai means *Lord* in Hebrew. Thus, when the English translators translated the Old Testament, they translated the word *Lord* instead of YHWH. They translated how it was spoken rather than how it was written. Since vowels were not put in the original Hebrew text, and since no one dared pronounce God's Name at the time vowels were put into the Hebrew text, no one knows how to pronounce God's Name.

In ancient Hebrew custom, God's Name could only be pronounced once a year, by only one person, and that would be by the High Priest, at Yom Kippur the Day of Atonement.

While this practice by the Jewish faith certainly keeps the Name holy, we of the non-Jewish persuasion, might think this is a little extreme. After all, the bible does not prohibit the pronouncing of the Name, but rather only the avoidance of making it worthless.

In fact, some verses seem to command that we use it. For instance, in Proverbs 18:10 it states *The Name of the Lord is a strong tower and the righteous run into it and are safe.* And in Romans 10:13, *For everyone who calls on the Name of the Lord will be saved.*

How can we call on the Name if we are afraid to say it? If we can call on the Name of the Lord, how can we do so in a way that does not make the Name of the Lord worthless?

One way to misuse the Name or to make it worthless, is *not giving it the respect it is due.* Using His Name as a cuss word is obvious. That's what I used to think the Third Commandment meant. So many do use God's name as a cuss word, and we can call God's Name in other speech expressions as, "Oh Lord," and the like, without actually, cussing, but really we are not praying either. We are merely using His name as a statement of exasperation. Be careful to avoid this.

Calling God's Name is serious business and should only be done so in respectful prayer.

Other Christians misuse the Lord's Name in other ways. I have seen many Christians going about proclaiming, "The Lord says this, and God wants that" when really, it is obvious that such is what the individual speaker wants, and not necessarily what God wants.

Likewise, those who go about with words of prophecy and words of knowledge that may not really be from God, are associating His Name with error and falsehood.

Remember what the ancient penalty was for false prophecy? It would be wise not to use the Lord's name in a manipulative or loose-cannon fashion that is so popular in some church circles. Do not dare to say something is from the Lord unless it really is. Otherwise you are misusing the Name of the Lord.

The best way to avoid misusing the Name of the Lord is to keep it Holy. Just as Jesus instructs us to pray!

How Do We Keep a Name Holy?

Understanding holiness or sacredness is something that again we are unfamiliar with in the 21st Century Western world. Often to the extent that we think about holiness, we think that it is the absence of sin, but this is not really correct. Rather, if something is holy, it is something very special, only to be used on certain occasions, for a very specific purpose.

Something which is profane or common is the opposite of holy. It can be used for anything by any one at any time. We in America in the Evangelical churches have lost a sense of holiness. We abandoned it for familiarity and access. As I will describe later, this is out of balance.

To an American, the closest thing we have to something being sacred is the American flag. It is a mere piece of cloth with stripes and stars, yes, but it stands for something greater…the United States of America. When people see it, they think of our country and its ideals, not just the piece of colored cloth. As a result we have rules about how to treat a flag, when to fly it, when to salute it, and how to dispose of it when it is worn and has served its purpose.

At my law office, we have a flag which I fly when my office is open. But, we don't fly it if it is raining outside. Likewise, when it is dark we must take it in. When the flag gets old, we do not throw it in the garbage, but instead must burn it. All this should be done with respect, not for the cloth, but for what it symbolizes. By honoring the flag, we honor our country.

On the contrary if someone were to use the flag as a cloth to check the oil in their car, most people would rightly be offended. It would be okay to use other cloth, profane or common cloth for this purposes, but not the flag. The same is true when it comes to using the Name of the Lord.

The LORD is so much greater than the USA, He is the creator of the Universe, the Master of all things, and thus, we should treat His name with all the more respect!

THE BEST STEP WE CAN DO TO KEEP SOMETHING HOLY IS TO REMEMBER WHAT IT REPRESENTS!

What does the Name of God Represent? It represents the Creator of the Universe and all Life, the Alpha and the Omega, Redeemer of mankind, the Great Law Giver, the First Cause… Knowing WHO the Name of God represents, calls us to render that Name with the utmost respect. It is holy, it is set apart for a single purpose, and that purpose is to signify the Almighty and none other. It is holy. We must keep it so.

Holy Tension in the Lord's Prayer

When something is in tension, there are two forces pulling from each other, and yet still staying together. Another way to think of this is Mystery. Two seemingly contradictory ideas which, while opposite, are both somehow true.

The Christian religion is truly not a religion of easy answers or black and white concepts. Rather, it is a religion of Mystery. If you want easy answers, the true faith is not the place to look for it.

Think about the Mysteries of the Christian religion. We believe God to be a Trinity, three persons, each separate, and yet making up one whole. We believe in the incarnation, where a transcendent God that is *omni* present, all powerful, and all knowing, somehow became a baby born to common people, Joseph and Mary, and this baby was truly God and truly man.

Likewise, when we think about the character of God, He is at once an Almighty, all powerful righteous judge, and at the same time a merciful God abounding in grace. This tension is brought out in the first line of the Lord's Prayer. When we pray, *Our FATHER who art in heaven HALLOWED BE THY NAME* we are thinking of two seemingly opposite concepts at the same time. Jesus is teaching us to be aware of a holy tension.

When we pray the word *Father* we think of the closeness, love, affection, friendship of an ACCESSIBLE God. Elsewhere in the Bible we call him…*abba or daddy*. When we think of God as Father, we think of mercy and love and tenderness.

However, when we pray *Hallowed be thy Name*, we are reminded that we are dealing with the everlasting God, Creator of the Universe, who judges the sin of mankind in righteousness. This is the God who has destroyed the entire world as well as peoples who have refused to repent of their sins, and promises to do so once again with fire, during the Apocalypse!

Being the imperfect mortals that we are, we have a difficult time holding these two equally true, but seemingly opposite conceptions of God in balance.

Muslims, on one hand, have no problem imagining a holy God who destroys sin, but they have a hard time seeing God as their loving Father who wants to be their friend.

On the other hand, liberal Protestants are quite comfortable with the *lovey-dovey fuzzy Father/Abba God*, who is so full of mercy, that He is incapable of even defining sin, much less punishing sin and holding people accountable, because they might be offended. Yet God is both of these things, and more.

In the Lord's Prayer, we begin our prayer with a single line bringing these two seemingly opposing forces together. We are reminded in the phrase *Our Father who art in heaven Holy is your Name or Hallowed be thy Name*…that while God is our buddy, and our daddy, He is also fearsome and to be respected.

For those of you familiar with C.S. Lewis and his <u>Chronicles of Narnia</u>, this point is brought out quite well. In <u>The Lion, the Witch, and the Wardrobe</u>, the lion Aslan represents Jesus Christ, who sacrifices his own life on the stone table, for the sins of Edmund, and through his death, he breaks the stone table and the power of the White Witch.

Edmund's sister Lucy, is especially attached to the Lion and there is a scene where Lucy deals with the paradox of Aslan's character. While she loves Aslan and she wants to hug and kiss him, she must also deal with the fact that he is *not a tame lion* and *not a kitty cat.*

While Aslan acts loving toward the children, he takes no thought to destroying his enemies, the forces of darkness, in battle.

Likewise, while God is loving and merciful, He is also righteous. He is also Almighty, and in the Great Battle to come, He will destroy the forces of darkness and its human followers. He is *not a tame lion*, but the Lion of Judah.

I mentioned earlier that our worship was out of balance. My opinion is that in the Protestant Evangelical Church we often emphasize the accessibility of God so much that we forget His holiness. We preach about grace, and tell everyone to come as they are, and we remember Jesus as our friend, and this is all true. But we often lack the feeling that we are entering Holy Ground when we go to our sanctuaries. We don't want God to be inaccessible to the seeker, yet we must remember that He is a holy God, and the worship of God is a serious business. Let us remember that He is *not a tame lion.* Let us remember that Holy Tension.

There is Power in the Name of the Lord

There is a famous old song called, <u>There is Power in the Name of the Lord</u>. Yes there is.

When the Name of the Lord is treated with respect and kept holy, there is great power in this name. The Bible reveals that Abraham prayed to the Name of the Lord, so did Isaac. The Lord first revealed his Name to Moses in the burning bush, where He appointed Moses to save the Israelites from bondage in Egypt. When Moses demanded to know who he should say sent him, the LORD replied, "I am who I am. Say 'I AM' has sent me to you."

When we call on the Name of the Lord, we are invoking His presence in a special way. Of course, He is always present in actuality, but He is not present in our MINDS until we call His Name. In Proverbs 18:10, the writer declares, *The Name of the Lord is a strong tower and the righteous run into it and are safe.*

Indeed, the Name of the Lord protects us, like a strong tower. He preserves our life, when we run into His embrace. When we call upon the Name of the Lord, we are calling the Lord to us.

Of course the Lord is everywhere, but that doesn't mean we are always thinking of Him, or accessing His power. When we invoke THE NAME OF THE LORD we are remembering who we are, and who protects us, and we are calling on that God to save us!

Romans 10:13 declares *For everyone who calls on the Name of the Lord will be saved.*

Is the Name, itself, a magical word, or an incantation?

No! But the God who lies behind it is a God who can do all things. When we say the Name of the Lord, no matter which language we use, we are calling God to our side. He is everywhere, but we are not aware of it.

Think of a computer. It is full of information, but unless we use certain words on the key board, the computer will not bring up the information on the screen, even though it is there on the hard drive.

Likewise, anyone in the world who has a cell phone is on the network, and present to you in a certain way, but unless you punch in their individual number, you will not hear their voice.

The Name of the Lord is like that computer program, or that telephone number. It brings us into awareness of the presence of the LORD. When we MISUSE the Name of the Lord, it is like *mis-programming* the computer so that other thoughts and other information might come to mind instead of that which the Great Programmer intended.

The Name of the LORD is a great power, not to be used as a spell or incantation to bring to us what WE desire, but rather to bring us into the Presence of the Almighty to receive what HE desires.

And what does God desire?

God wants to save us–if we will only come to Him. God is always willing to save, to comfort and to love, and often willing to heal, to rescue, and rebuild–if we will only ask Him.

If you are broken hearted–God wants to mend that heart.

If you are caught in the bondage of sin–God wants to deliver you.

If you are sick–He may want to cure you.

If you are in trouble–He wants you to give Him a chance to rescue you.

God wants to heal…

He wants to deliver…

He wants to comfort…

He wants to save…

His Name IS a strong tower and the righteous run into it, and are saved.

Call

The Bible says, *If my people, who are called by my Name, will humble themselves and pray and seek my face and turn from their wicked ways, then will I hear from heaven and will forgive their sin and heal their land. 2 Chronicles 7:14.*

We've seen this a million times in calls for revival….my question is this. If we are called by God's Name, and we don't repent of our wicked ways, what kind of name and reputation are we giving God? Are we misusing the Name of God by giving Him a bad reputation to those who don't know God, but DO know us as the people of God?

Let u call upon our Father in Heaven knowing all the love and affection and grace that represents. Let us also declare Holy is Your name to remind ourselves that He is also the fearsome creator and judge. He is our Beloved.

We must respect and obey Him and never lose sight of that holy tension.

In our Hearts, and in our Church, Oh Father God, Let your Name be made Holy, indeed!

Reflections:

HALLOWED BY THY NAME

In the church you attend, is the holiness of God stressed, or the accessibility of God? Do you think this is a good balance? How could things be changed to put the attributes of God more in balance?

Do you think God cares if you sin? If you believe you are saved, what is the probable result of your sin?

How should the holiness of God affect our walk with Him? What makes something holy?

Do you ever misuse God's Name? In what ways? How could you change this?

THY KINGDOM COME,
THY WILL BE DONE
ON EARTH AS IT IS IN HEAVEN

The kingdom of God does not come with careful observation, nor will people say, 'Here it is or there it is,' because the kingdom of God is within you. Luke 17:20-21.

When *The Lord's Prayer* is read, many people can follow along aloud. We do this because it is one we know it by heart. Most of us were taught to recite *The Lord's Prayer* by memory when we were children. Why is it so important?

During the Sermon on the Mount, an individual asked our Lord Jesus how we should pray, and these are the words He gave us!

We pray this prayer in liturgy during our services, and some of us pray this prayer at home exactly or at least use it as a model as we fashion our individual prayers.

The second verse of the prayer is *Thy Kingdom Come, Thy will be done–on earth as it is in heaven*. What does it mean?

What are we praying for exactly, when we pray these words?

The words refer to the Kingdom of God, or alternatively phrased, the Kingdom of Heaven.

I used to think that the Kingdom of Heaven was what happened after we were dead and in heaven, and that the Kingdom of God was what happened after the Second Coming of Christ. If this is true, then we would be praying for our swift deaths, or the soon destruction of the world. Now I understand that we are asking for God's rule to come here on earth right now, not later, so that His will shall be done the same here as in heaven.

To understand what this means, we need to understand, *what is the Kingdom of God?*

What Is the Kingdom of God?

Jesus mentions and teaches on it 72 times in the Gospels, more times than he mentions eternal life, and while His teachings focus on the Kingdom of God, most of us don't understand it, or focus on it. In our faith, instead, we turn our attention to the question of how we can attain eternal life.

This reminds me of a story, which I'm almost sure is a joke, but it illustrates a point:

There was an 80 year old woman who became news-worthy when she married her fourth husband. As she was being interviewed, the reporter asked her what her husband did for a living, and she replied that he was an undertaker. The reporter then asked about her previous husbands and their occupations.

She related that the first was a banker whom she married in her 20's, the second was a circus performer whom she married in her 40's, the third was a pastor whom she married in her 60's.

"Wow!" The reporter said. "That's quite a variety of men you've shared your life with over the decades! Did they have anything in common, any particular theme which they shared?"

"Yes," replied the old woman, "I married the first for the money, the second for the show, the third to get ready, and the fourth to go!"

This humorous story illustrates an attitude that most people have about Christianity, which is that we adopt faith to *get ready*. Get ready for what?

To die! So we'll go to heaven and not to hell.

Many preachers spend the vast majority of their preaching time on this question. "How you can be saved, so you'll go to heaven after you die." For this reason, Christianity has always been more attractive to old people than to young.

Old people are thinking about *End of Life* questions, and want to make sure their ducks are in a row, so that when the time comes, they'll have confidence that they are going to a good place after death. Many of these old people did not attend church when they were young, but are quite faithful in their old age.

The young, on the other hand, are rarely thinking about death. To them, they want to think about life, not death.

A Christianity which is merely a *life insurance policy* can wait till later. This doesn't describe everyone, of course, but illustrates a major problem in reaching out to young adults. If we continue focusing on "How do we achieve eternal life," questions, we are only going to reach a select portion of the population worried about such questions.

Jesus, in His preaching certainly stated quite famously in *John 3:16 For God so loved the world, that He gave His only begotten Son, so that whosoever believeth in Him shall not perish, but have everlasting life!"* And likewise, *"I am come that they might have life, and that they might have it more abundantly." John 10:10.*

Jesus did not come only to teach about what happens after we die. He came to teach us not about how to die, but how to live! He came to proclaim the institution of His Kingdom, the Kingdom of God, not 2000 years away, or only after you are dead, but right now while you are alive!

He proclaimed, *Repent for the Kingdom of God is at hand!* That means right now. Not later. Furthermore, eternal life is eternal, that means it is now as well as in the future.

Likewise, abundant life, is what we have now as well as in the future.

Jesus came to teach us how to live, and how to join His Kingdom, His family, right now!

I like to think of our *Sinners Prayer* as not just signing a life insurance contract where we are congratulated on our good *decision* and then can put it away in the kitchen drawer and forget about it. Rather, when we pray for Jesus to become Savior and Lord of our lives, we are signing an Enlistment Contract.

When we join the Army, we do not just put our enlistment papers away, but rather we put on a uniform and begin a life of service to accomplish whatever mission our commander gives us.

As new Christians, we are enlisting our service to the Lord of the Universe to accomplish His mission. And what is His mission? It is to establish His Kingdom on Earth as it is in heaven. You may ask, "Isn't God already the ruler of the Universe? Why does He need to establish His Kingdom?"

I think of the example of Mainland China and Taiwan. For those of you who read the newspaper or know history, in 1949, Mainland China was taken by the Communists and the Nationalists retreated to the Island of Taiwan. In Mainland China, there is one party rule under the Communists, and in Taiwan there is a Democratic Government. Mainland China says it is the ruler of all China including the Island of Taiwan.

The United Nations has said that Taiwan is ruled by Mainland China, and even the United States acknowledges that Mainland China is the ruler of Taiwan. But in reality, the people of Taiwan rule in Taiwan, and no laws passed in Mainland China are enforced in Taiwan. Mainland China is the legal ruler of Taiwan, but not the actual ruler of Taiwan.

Likewise, God rules the entire Universe, including the earth. But He gave us *free will* to choose to follow Him or not. Since the Garden of Eden, mankind has been in rebellion against the rule of God, and we have felt the consequences of our rebellion, our sin. Death, destruction, brokenness, famine, loneliness, anger, greed, poverty, war and violence rule our lives, due to our sin.

God wants to work through our free choice to retake this land, and to restore His righteous rule over a consenting population. He wants to restore, love, peace, forgiveness, joy, equality, health and tranquility that are the natural results of following His rule. He has enlisted you and I, Christian, to help Him accomplish this goal! The Kingdom of God is wherever, and in whomever, God's will is being done by God's people.

How do we establish the Kingdom of God?

The Kingdom of God is needs to be established on earth as well as in heaven. It must be established in our individual souls as well as the community around us.

You can often tell a liberal church from a conservative one, by the values and commands of God that they emphasize, as well as the ones that they ignore.

I grew up in a conservative church. When I was sixteen, God inspired me to become active in helping the *Vietnamese Boat People*. I was so excited to help people poorer than myself, and I approached the Pastor and asked for permission to get the Church involved in my proposed mission project to the poor of our local community. He turned me down, saying, "We don't believe in the Social Gospel. We need to spend what few resources we have in teaching the Word of God, so that people can be saved." I didn't argue with him, because I was only sixteen, but I left the church thinking, "*Didn't Jesus do both?*"

As I got older, I became active with a more liberal church. They helped me with an after school Youth Program for South East Asian kids, and I went to their Missions program where we had a chance to deliver our pitch for funds. Program after program came up to share their projects, and finally we had our chance, AND WE WERE THE ONLY ONES IN THAT WHOLE MISSIONS CONFERENCE TO MENTION THE NAME JESUS OR TO STATE THAT EVANGELISM WAS ONE OF OUR GOALS!

People! The Kingdom of God is where God is in charge of our individual hearts, and that only comes through Evangelism and proclaiming the word of God. It also comes where these people of God then go out into the world through temporal as well as spiritual actions, and do God's will on the earth here and now!

This requires *Social Action, politics, organization and money.* We need to do both; Spirit and flesh. Didn't Jesus say that we are the *Salt of the Earth? Matt. 5:13.* Didn't He say that we are *the Light of the World? Matt 5:14.* Wasn't Jesus Himself a miracle of the divine being united with the material, fully God and fully man?

Likewise, the Kingdom of God must be a reflection of our Savior, both a spiritual rebirth, as well as direct action, here on earth.

How do we establish the Kingdom of God in the world? First, we start with our hearts.

God needs to rule in your life. Is He in charge right now? Have you submitted your whole life to His rule or are you still holding on to parts?

You need to understand, that if you are going to claim the Name of Jesus, you are offering yourself and your whole life first and foremost. You'll be amazed at how much better the world around you will be, if you'll allow God to work with you in cleaning up your own life first. There may be your family to save, your friends and acquaintances who can be positively affected by a YOU that follows the teachings of God instead of the laws of sin and selfishness. As people see your life change under the rule of God, you will be the Light of the World.

But don't stop there, and don't fall for the trap that you must be perfect before you move on. You will never be perfect. You will never succeed in entirely yielding your life to God, or getting rid of sin. If you could, you would not need a Savior. We are saved by God's grace, through faith in Jesus Christ, and He had to die on the cross, because we cannot be saved through our own self effort, or our own holiness.

Despite this, we are compelled to give this incomplete work our utmost, because it is part of our mission to establish God's Kingdom on Earth as well as in heaven. Our hearts are on earth, and the most under our control, so we start here.

Simultaneously, as we are working on our own lives, we should be looking around to see where we can contribute to the establishment of God's kingdom. Where do you see brokenness, sadness, hunger or injustice? These are all places you can start!

Feed the hungry, contribute to disaster relief, comfort the mourning, visit the prisoners, clothe the naked…there is so much need, and so few resources to meet the need. Where can you help? As you pray, the prayer *Thy Kingdom Come, Thy will be done on Earth as it is in Heaven…* Ask the Holy Spirit to specifically guide you where he wants you to get involved. If you don't feel the guidance yet, meet the needs immediately before and around you.

Trust me, you will never be able to meet all the need of this world. Neither will all the Christians on earth, even if we were doing what we are supposed to. That is why the world needs a Savior. Until Christ returns, we will never solve all the problems, but that is no excuse to not try and do our best to solve what we can, and to establish God's kingdom, now, where we are able. We can make change one moment at a time.

Historically, how have we done, since the coming of Christ?

Some may think that the teachings of Jesus are so *pie in the sky* that they have made no difference. If so, they are wrong. What have Christians accomplished over the last 2000 years?

Billions of lives have found meaning where before they had none, as countless millions of prostitutes, thieves, killers, gangsters, drug users, wife beaters, and drug addicts have changed their individual lives after coming to Christ.

We have seen the establishment of hospitals, where before there were none; the establishment of universities for the common man, where before they were reserved to the rich; the abolishment of legalized human slavery; the idea that women and children are loved by God and just as important as powerful men, is a uniquely Judeo Christian concept.

We have accepted the concept that each person has worth before God, which led to the establishment of the concept of Democracy; the feeding of millions of people in Africa and India and other places where people are poor and starving; and the concept that humility is a virtue.

All of these things came about into human history as a result of Christian ideas and Christian influence. The world really is a better place than it was 2000 years ago, but we still have a long ways to go!

Who Is God Seeking?

God is looking for a few good men and women to enlist in His Kingdom service, to seize this life, here and now to establish His will on Earth as well as in heaven. Jesus said,

No one who puts his hand to the plow and looks back is fit for service in the Kingdom of God." Luke 9:62. He wants committed servants, who will offer up more than a half-hearted struggle.

Believe me, if we adopt this attitude, we will have fewer problems in evangelism and fewer problems retaining the youth of our church. When young people see a group of Christians who are personally striving for holiness, going out to serve the poor, right the wrongs, and do justice, they will be excited. They will want to join. They will not want to join a group of old people who are *getting ready to die* so they can enjoy their eternal reward.

That said, let me tell you something about the Army of God. Not only is service in this Army exciting! Not only are the goals always just. Not only will you be making the world a better place to live. Not only will your life become more meaningful as you put into practice the teachings of the Divine Master of the Universe, but this Army has a great retirement plan. Yes! The old people are right too. When we participate in the Kingdom of God, it is not only for this Life. It is not for days, years, or decades, but for all eternity!

As the old song goes, When we've been there, 10,000 years, we've no less days to sing his praise, than when we've first begun! Jesus came so that we could have life. Life eternal. Life to its fullest. That means right now, not later, but it also means later and forever.

Call

Will you join up? Will you join this struggle for a better future right now? If you have yet to give your life to Christ, today is the day! He wants You!It starts with a decision and a promise, and continues with a life devoted.

Dear Lord, today, we pray *Thy Kingdom Come, Thy will be done, on Earth as it is in heaven!*

Reflections:

THY KINGDOM COME, THY WILL BE DONE ON EARTH AS IT IS IN HEAVEN

1. When you look around at the people you deal with on a daily basis, who do you see could benefit from more of God's love? What could you do to bring that love?

2. Have you ever felt prompted to give or provide some help, and the recipient tells you that they were praying for that help?

3. Have you ever felt prompted to help, and ignored that prompting? Why did you ignore it? What were your reasons? How can you describe that prompting?

4. When you are helping people less fortunate, is it necessary to tell them about the Gospel as you are doing it? What is the advantage of doing this? What is the drawback? What is a good balance? Can the Kingdom of God be spread by simple acts without words? Why or why not?

5. What is something that your church could do right now in the community that would make a material difference in the life of others? Would you be willing to lead or fund such an effort through your own resources?

GIVE US THIS DAY OUR DAILY BREAD

When Jesus was asked by His disciples to teach them to pray, he began with celestial matters such as realizing the Fatherhood of God, making God's Name Holy, and instituting the Kingdom of God. He quickly turned to more mundane matters. As His attention turns from Heaven to Earth, He utters the words, *Give us this day our daily bread.*

Back in the First Century, getting something to eat was a pressing matter. But does this prayer have any meaning for modern 21st Century America? After all, food is both abundant and cheap in this country.

Have any of you ever gone hungry? Have any of you ever known anyone personally who has starved to death? I know I haven't. How is this prayer even relevant to us today? Why do we, in 21st Century America need to pray for our daily bread?

God's word is relevant to all people for all time. As I prayed about this question in preparation for this chapter, the Holy Spirit gave me three words to share with you.

These three words display the relevance of this short prayer

1) Humility

2) Faith

3) Generosity

Humility

What about humility? Jesus teaches us to pray for our necessities whether we are in need or not. Why? To teach us humility.

While you may think that you have food because of your great skill, education, and hard work, do you realize how quickly all that could become nothing? Your skill, education and hard work are still dependent on your health. How quickly would your personal empire collapse if you got cancer, became blind, or disabled?

Your skill, education, hard work also depend on the weather and peace in civil society. Look at the East Coast and our most recent Hurricane Sandy. With a single storm, New York and much of the Eastern Seaboard lost electricity, saw its roads and subways flooded, and food and gasoline quickly fell into short supply.

The truth is, despite all your hard work and skill, so much depends on others and on so called Acts of God. The truth is, everything you have and depend on could be wiped out in a few days by war, famine, storm, pestilence or illness.

When Jesus commands us, who have so much, to pray for our daily bread, it is to remind us, that inevitably everything comes from God. This is to remind us of humility. When it gets down to it, "We didn't really build that."

Let me use a different example. If any of you have kids, or remember when you were a kid, you have encountered the situation where the kid asks the parent for something which the parent wants to give, but not for free. Instead, the parent says something like, "*Okay, if you want that bicycle, you've gotta do some chores for me over the next few weeks.*"

The kid agrees, and does the chores. He gets the bicycle. The kid thinks he earned the bicycle, but the reality is, the money came from the loving parent who wanted to provide that bike.

So it is with us and God. God is the source of all our provision. As we pray, *Give us this day our daily bread*, we are reminded of the True Source of our daily existence. As we remember this, let us thank Him!

The Prayer also says, *Give us this day OUR daily bread.*

When praying this prayer, we are not encouraged to be lazy. While God is the source of our existence, we also need to cooperate through our labor and hard work. We are not simply to lay back in laziness with the comment, "*God will provide.*" Yes, He will provide us OUR daily bread–that which we work for. Not someone else's daily bread, but OURS.

Paul faced this situation in the early church, when people thought the Lord was going to return any day, and they quit their jobs and leaned back on the generosity of other Christians. Paul saw that they were being lazy and taking advantage, so he wrote the Thessalonian Church, *If a man will not work, neither shall he eat. I Thess. 3:10.*

A little later in Matthew, Chapter 6, Jesus, in commanding his disciples not to worry, tells them to look to the birds who neither toil nor spin but are still provided for by the Father, but if we are honest, birds are not lazy either. They wake up at the crack of dawn to wait for the worm, and if they stay up too late the night before drinking beer, they will miss the worm and go hungry. Furthermore, they are quite busy building nests, and flying north and south to beat the weather!

Going back to my example of the kid and his loving parent, if after the parent offers to provide the bicycle in exchange for a few weeks of chores, the kid were to turn around and say, "*No thanks, I know you'll give it to me anyway!*" A good parent will deny that little ingrate a bike!

No, we are not to be lazy when praying for our daily bread. Rather we are to cooperate with God and do our best, and then He will make up the rest!

Faith

The second word I wish you to remember about this prayer is "Faith". Now, while none of you here have ever starved to death, or known anyone who has, how many of you have been worried about loss of a job? How many have worried about losing your house or your car? How many have wondered whether you would be able to eat? Yes, quite a lot of you have been in this situation and still are.

Financial uncertainty is quite common in this life. Jesus is teaching us to depend on God in this situation. Interestingly, the bread we are commanded to pray for, is *epiousion* in the Greek, which means *for our existence*

There are other things we need *for our existence* as well as food, such as clothes and shelter. For many of us, providing for these things is a little more tricky, and we can and should go to God with these needs.

Now, what we *need* and what we *want* are often two different things! I am willing to state unequivocally that while a teenager WANTS a smart phone, they do not NEED one. Contrary to what they might believe, if we lost our smart phones, none of us would die!

Likewise, we do not NEED one car for each person in the house, or cable TV, or internet, or any of the many luxuries that we have become so accustomed to.

A visit to Vietnam or Mexico will quickly educate you on the difference between what you NEED and what you WANT. God will provide for your *needs*, but not necessarily for your *greeds*.

In Matthew 6:25-34, Jesus was teaching his disciples not to worry. He told them to consider the lilies of the field and the birds of the air, and the fact that God in heaven provided for these creatures. Instead, He commanded us to seek first the Kingdom of God, and all these things would be added unto us. But honestly, worrying is something that comes quite naturally to us when we are faced with uncertainty.

When I was in the sixth grade, I went to Camp. Some of you have been to sixth grade camp, haven't you? Well, in the sixth grade, I was voted *Worry Wart of the Camp*. I can't help worrying. As an intelligent person, I can lay out a hundred scenarios of how things could go wrong and I could be in a lot of trouble. But Jesus tells us not to worry.

How can we do that when faced with hunger, unemployment, financial trouble? The answer is faith.

Faith is the opposite of Worry. To the extent we have faith, that is the extent that worrying is extinguished. How do we have faith? By praying! We bring our worries to God, and ask Him to provide. *Give us this day our daily bread.* When we pray, we overcome worry.

I remember, about ten years ago, there was an Initiative on the ballot that if passed would have wiped out my business. If that happened, I would have had to close my office and sell my house. What could I do? I would worry, and then I would pray and feel better. ... and then about an hour later, I would worry again, then I would pray, then I would worry.

Every time I prayed I felt better because I knew that my future was in the hands of God who loved me. Likewise, the Father loves you, and He will provide for your necessities. Maybe not all your *wants*, but your *necessities*.

We are told to pray for our daily bread, because we ought to be going to the Father with our needs and wants at least on a daily basis. This prayer is a faith building prayer. We can cease worrying because when we pray this prayer, we can believe in a God who loves us and provides.

I have a friend who has impressed me with his faith. He is married with five kids, and lives on only one income while his wife home-schools the kids. He lost his job, and then was injured, and then after getting another job, had his hours cut back.

He really does live day-to-day, and often doesn't know how he is going to put gas in the car, or put a meal on the table the next day. He told me, he wasn't worried. He believed God would provide as He always has. He went on to say, "I believe God is just using these circumstances to teach me how to live with less in order to prepare me for the work He has for me!" Now that is faith. Trust in God. He loves you. He will provide.

Are you having a hard time? This prayer teaches you that God is listening. He wants you to come to him with your economic troubles. You do not have to be saintly by only praying for others. Pray for your own necessities of life as well. Take it to the Lord and trust in Him.

Generosity

The third word that I want you to consider when remembering this prayer is "generosity". The sad thing is, that in this world, despite the prayer, *give us this day our daily bread*, many still go hungry, and there are people in other countries who do starve to death.

In fact, according to world hunger organizations, there are 5 million children a year who die of hunger related issues. According to the United Nations Food & Agriculture Organization, in 2010 up to 925 million people are *malnourished*. This is about 1/6 of the world's population!

Some say, this is the result of over-population; that there isn't enough food to go around. Wrong. Statistics show that there is enough food grown for every person to eat 2700 calories a day. Nutritionists say we only need between 1200 and 1800. Some of us, of course look like we do eat our entire 2700 calories, but the truth is, there is more than enough food to go around. We don't have a production problem—we have a distribution problem.

Going back to the five million children who die of hunger—many of these kids are Christians in Africa and Asia, and they pray this prayer, *give us this day our daily bread* and yet they still starve to death. Is this God's fault? Is He not listening? Does He lack the power to provide? Or is it our problem, because we are not listening to the promptings of the Holy Spirit to do more for these unfortunates?

"I am poor, and don't have enough to share," you say. Let me tell you, if you live in America, you are rich even if you are on welfare. The average welfare recipient has money to live in an apartment with a roof and four walls, heating and air conditioning, hot and cold running water, electricity, access to a public transportation system and law enforcement. They have food stamps, and medical treatment provided by Medi-Cal and money in their pocket.

Many in the world literally have none of these things. Do you know how much money it would take to feed 5 million starving kids? I figured it out. If every Christian gave ½ cent a day, there would be enough! Can you afford that?

Don't get me wrong. It is not that Christians are oblivious to the Holy Spirit. A simple review of organizations providing food to the hungry of the world, shows that a vast majority of them are Christian charities. Things would be a lot worse were it not for the good work of these Christians and their donors who do listen to the Holy Spirit. I am just saying that since the problem still exists, we need to do more. We need to listen more.

There are times that God will present opportunities to you right here in your neighborhood to provide a helping hand. My neighbor drove to work one day and saw a black teenage boy on her porch, and as it was still dark outside, she was somewhat afraid. She asked him, "Can I help you." And he replied, "Move on!"

She was even more afraid and did not want to walk up the porch by herself, and so she waited for another co-worker to arrive and the two of them approached the young man again. It turned out that his clothes were wet and he had been sleeping outside and sought the porch for protection. He was homeless, stating that his mom could not afford to care for him anymore.

In the end, my neighbor gave him money for breakfast, because he hadn't eaten in a while. While she initially was afraid of this young man, she finally listened to the Holy Spirit and responded to him in charity rather than fear.

Are we not the hands and feet of Christ on this earth? *Need* exists all around us. Individuals are praying, *Give us this day our daily bread*, and by and large, God will answer these prayers through us. While miracles and angels exist, most miracles happen because we listen to the promptings of the Holy Spirit and respond through generosity.

Conclusion

Ladies and Gentlemen, the Lord's Prayer is such a simple prayer. Tucked into it are the simple words, *Give us this day our daily bread.*

As we pray this prayer, let us remember:

1)Humility. We are all in need of God's provision. All goodness comes from Him. Let us be thankful.

2)Faith… if we are uncertain or anxious…Let us take our needs to the Lord, and He will be faithful to provide.

3)Generosity…whatever you think your economic situation, there are many others who are worse. Be open to the guidance and the prompting of the Holy Spirit to reach out in generosity and love when confronted by the need of others…

Reflections:

GIVE US THIS DAY OUR DAILY BREAD

1. In what ways did you earn your current success and create the lifestyle you now lead?

2. What kinds of things could happen that would destroy you financially in a very short time. What kinds of financial issues worry you? Unemployment, disability, retirement? Changes in the economy? How do you deal with these worries? Can prayer help?

3. When you see others suffering economically, do you tend to blame them for creating their own problems? Do you feel sorry for them? Do you pray for them? Do you do anything else to alleviate the trouble you see? What could you do?

4. Do we as Christians have any responsibility to assist God in answering the call of other Christians for their daily bread? If so, what can we do? Will you pray that the Holy Spirit will assist you to be more willing to see trouble and act to help?

?

FORGIVE US OUR DEBTS, AS WE FORGIVE OUR DEBTORS

What Should You Do When People Hurt You?

How many of you have ever been hurt by another?

How many have had a friend stab you in the back?

How many of you have had an enemy really get one over on you?

How many have been the victim of malicious gossip, or been disappointed by a spouse or a child?

We've all been in these situations and the pain we receive is very real! We truly are the victims. But what does the Bible say about how we should handle this pain?

When we are hurt, the flesh tells us either to withdraw and nurse our pain by avoiding the perpetrator or giving him/her the silent treatment, or in the alternative, the flesh wants us to calculate how to get our revenge. Revenge is sweet!

Right? People who get revenge will tell you, it doesn't solve anything. The pain from the original injury is still there.

I once knew a lady who told me, "*If anyone ever crosses me, even once, I'm burning that bridge. They'll never get to me again!*"

I told her, "If you burn all your bridges, you'll be on an island all by yourself." Indeed, that is how she lived.

I knew another lady who would tell her husband, "That's just one more thing on my list!" every time he did something to annoy her.

I told her, "Throw away that list, or you'll have to get rid of your husband." About five years later, she got rid of her husband.

Both of these ladies believe in Jesus Christ, but their conduct was directly opposite to what Christ has demanded of us in the Scripture readings, today.

With regard to the list and the lost husband, I am reminded of Psalm 130, where the psalmist declares to God, *If you O LORD, kept a record of sins, O LORD, who could stand? But with You there is forgiveness; therefore You are feared. Psalm 130:3-4.*

Christian, if your husband or wife kept a list of every wrong thing you ever did, every time you disappointed, who of you could keep your marriage?

If you did this to your friends, how long could your relationship last? There is only so much paper on our lists, and eventually, with the passage of time, we will all get to the bottom.

How about our relationship with God? How many times a day do we sin, by either doing something wrong in our actions, deeds or thoughts? How many times do we fail to do what we know we should? If God kept account of all of this, how many of us could look forward to salvation?

This is why Jesus Christ came to earth. This is why He consented to be stripped naked, spat upon, maligned and insulted. This is why He allowed Himself to be nailed to a cross and killed. He did this so that God could fully and finally throw away that list. He did this, so that He could offer us true and complete forgiveness. He demands of us, the same thing that He did for us. We must forgive.

Forgiveness Is Not Optional

Jesus gave us the parable of the unmerciful servant as He described how we must conduct ourselves as Christians. He told a story of a Master and a Servant. This servant was greatly indebted to the Master. He owed the equivalent of millions of dollars, and there was no way the servant could repay.

Now, back then, they did not have Chapter 7 bankruptcy. If you owed money you could not repay, your creditors had the right to sell you and your family into slavery to repay the debt, or even more cruelly, put you into a debtor's prison, to be mistreated until your friends and loved ones raised enough money to repay the debt and get you out!

While the master intended to have the servant and his family sold into slavery, he was touched by compassion towards the servant who was pleading for more time.

Realistically, the servant would require thousands of years to repay such a large sum, so instead, the Master said, "Just forget about it. Your debts are forgiven!"

He didn't just refinance the debt, but told the servant he was free of the obligation. No more debt. No more prospect of slavery. Freedom!

Now, if the parable stopped here, we would have a good picture of what God has done for us. Due to our sin, we owed Him a great debt that we never in our lifetimes could repay, but God in His Mercy incarnated His Son, Jesus, to become Man, and pay the price on our behalf. We are freed of the debt of sin, and saved from the prospect of slavery, and instead given freedom in Christ Jesus. What rapture, what joy we should feel when thinking on this. Just like that servant must have felt. But, no–the parable doesn't end here.

The forgiven servant, himself, was owed money by a fellow servant. This fellow owed the equivalent of about three-month's salary. Even though the forgiven servant was just freed of this large debt, he went to his fellow and grabbed his neck demanding immediate repayment.

When the fellow servant begged for more time, just as the forgiven servant had done, the forgiven servant not only failed to act as his master had done, but instead had the fellow servant thrown into debtor's prison. When word of this got back to the Master, the Master was infuriated. So much so, that he had the forgiven servant thrown into prison until ALL his debt should be repaid. Since this could never be done, this was the equivalent of a life sentence.

Why was the Master infuriated? The forgiven servant had the legal right to act as he did to the fellow servant. The forgiven servant was not acting dishonestly. The fellow servant really owed the money, and the man really didn't pay it back. No one in the world could blame the forgiven servant. He was just doing justice under the laws of the time.

Christian, you and I are often in the same situation. When people have wronged us, all of our friends agree that the perpetrator is a real stinker. They all share in our anger toward the perpetrator, and encourage us in our anger, and even in our desire for revenge. "Don't let that so and so get away with this! You go girl/guy!"

When we are the victims, sometimes it is due to our own fault, or our own misunderstanding, but many times, we are really innocent victims.

What does the Bible say we should do when we are wronged?

The Master did not question whether the forgiven servant was really owed the money, or whether he had abused the legal process. What upset the Master was that, as a FORGIVEN servant, he did not *pay it forward*.

As Christians, we are not called to stand on our rights, but we are called to stand on our Faith in Jesus Christ. We are called to pass on the mercy and love that we have received from the Master. And there will be horrible consequences if we refuse to pass it on.

In the parable, the Master cancelled His forgiveness of the previously forgiven servant. We are told not to read too much into parables, but this parable is followed by direct teaching from Jesus, as He explains the point. He warns, *This is how my heavenly Father will treat each of you, unless you forgive your brother from your heart. Matthew 18:35*

In teaching us how to pray, with the Lord's prayer, Jesus has us pray the following words, *Forgive us our debts, as we also have forgiven our debtors.*

If we pray this prayer, and yet are unwilling to forgive, we are praying judgment upon our own heads. In case we miss the point, Jesus again follows His Lord's Prayer with direct teaching. *For if you forgive men when they sin against you, your heavenly Father will also forgive you. But if you do not forgive men their sins, your Father will not forgive your sins. Matt. 6:14-15.*

These direct teachings from Christ tell us in no uncertain terms, that if you are to call yourself a Christian and expect forgiveness from God, then forgiveness from you to your fellow man **is not optional**! It is a required element of being a Christian. If you are not willing to follow Christ's example in this, then you do not have saving faith. End of story.

Some Christian theologians have problems with Jesus' teaching about such things. But if we are to be Christian theologians, then we need to take the words of Christ seriously. Here He teaches that forgiveness is not optional. We need to heed the words of Jesus Christ in this matter.

Forgiveness is Good For You

Laying aside the threat to your eternal soul, if you refuse to forgive, let's look at the here and now. I have said it before, and will repeat it today. The Holy Bible tells us how to live happy, joyful, and productive lives in the here and now. The Bible is God's ownership manual for His creation, man. Follow its instructions, and you will be happy. Ignore the instructions to your own peril.

Any secular psychologist will tell you that it is unhealthy to hold on to bitterness and un-forgiveness. Despite this common sense approach, it feels so good to be bitter doesn't it? We all love to be victims. We love to tell the story of how we have been wronged. We love to share with our friends how we have been victimized. We love to plot revenge.

Yet, despite how natural this is, it is exactly the wrong approach to our own long term happiness.

When I was younger, I was in the Army. I was not a very good soldier. I remember one incident in Boot Camp when we were learning how to throw hand grenades. I pulled the pin, but was so afraid that I hesitated to throw it. The drill sergeant quickly hit me on the helmet with an iron rod, attached a few profanities to my name, then grabbed the grenade and threw it over the wall himself. Then–BOOM!

Holding on to bitterness is like pulling the pin from a grenade and then being unwilling to get rid of it. If you hold on to it for too long, it will explode in your face, hurting you and those closest to you.

Forgiveness is like setting a prisoner free, and then realizing that prisoner is you. Bitterness is like a prison, but we are holding the door shut with our own power. Let go of the door, and you can go free!

It feels so good to nurse our hurt and our bitterness, but truthfully you are just hurting yourself, and honestly, the person against whom you hold a grudge probably doesn't even care. Have you ever given someone the silent period for a while, and then when you stopped, they weren't even aware that you were mad? Why don't we just stop and forgive? Well, many times we feel that we have a RIGHT to be angry. We are the VICTIM.

In the parable, the forgiven servant had a RIGHT to collect his money, but the Master didn't want him to stand on his RIGHTS. He wanted him to share the mercy he had himself received.

We also don't forgive because we don't love. David cried out, *Have mercy on me, O God, according to your unfailing love! Psalm 51:1*

God's mercy and forgiveness spring from His love. The reason we often forgive our children of their many wrongs, is because of our love for them. We have received God's love when we receive His forgiveness. Having received this love, we cannot hold onto it, and deny it to others; even our enemies. We are called on to love everyone, even our enemies. And from this love will spring forgiveness.

We also don't forgive, because we keep telling the story. We keep reminding ourselves of the wrong. We tell it again and again to anyone who will listen, and we play it again and again in our own minds. Have you ever known anyone like that? Have you been that person?

In Greek, the word for forgiveness is *Aphiemi* which literally means *To Let Go.*

Let it Go! The master in the parable knew he would never get back all the money he lost on the forgiven servant. He deemed it better to let it go. When we hold on to bitterness towards a person who has wronged us, every time we see that person or think of that person, we remember the wrong. We associate the sight or thought of that person with the wrong, and we keep feeling the pain again and again.

The Bible says God forgives *as far as the East is from the West, so far has He removed our transgressions from us. Psalm 103:12*

It's not that God has a bad case of Alzheimer's. It is that when God forgives us, He has chosen to stop associating us with the sin we have committed. Instead of seeing and remembering our sin, He remembers the person who He loves. We are called to love like this; To forget like this. To stop associating the person to the wrong they have committed. If we can do this, then we can forgive.

Forgiving Isn't Easy

"Fine," you say. "You have convinced me by the above threats and promises that I need to forgive, but forgiving isn't easy!"

No, it isn't. But being willing to try is the first step. Below, are some helpful pointers to help you forgive, if you want to try. Remember, since we are human, we really can't instantaneously forgive someone who has really hurt us. Forgiveness must come in layers. After peeling back each layer, we find another we need to deal with.

1. Focus on your own walk with God. Much of this has more to do with your own walk with God, than with your relationship with the perpetrator. In the great psalm of confession, David prayed, *Against you, and you only have I sinned.* Truth is, David also sinned greatly against Uriah. But that was passed. Now David was trying to focus on his relationship with God. Forgiving your perpetrator is essential to your own healthy relationship with God. With this in mind, begin with the following prayer, "For *Your sake*, help me to forgive Mr. X." At the beginning, you may not have ANY desire to forgive the wrongdoer, so make it about *your relationship with* God, instead.

2. Pray: "I forgive Mr. X, help me to mean it!" After you have forgiven Mr. X for *God's sake*, learn to say the words in prayer, even if your heart doesn't mean it. Ask for God's help to bring your heart along with the words of your confession.

3. For your own sake, try to forget the wrong. Start by Stop telling the story. Every very time you start to tell the story, catch yourself and stop. The wrongdoer victimized you once, long ago. But every time you bring up the story in your own mind, you are victimizing yourself with the pain all over again. Try to stop associating the person you are trying to forgive, with the wrong they committed.

4. Realize that it is God who serves Justice not you! So often we hold on to bitterness because we want to teach the wrong doer a lesson, and make sure he or she doesn't do it again. But Christian, it is not your duty to mete out God's justice by teaching lessons. Your job is to forgive. God says, *It is mine to avenge; I will repay says the Lord. Romans 12:16.* When WE try to mete out justice through our bitterness, we are attempting to takes God's power into our own hands, and show a lack of faith in God. Rather, we are commanded to do good to those who have harmed us. *If your enemy is hungry, feed him. If he is thirsty give him something to drink. In doing this you will heap burning coals on his head. Do not be overcome by evil, but overcome evil with good! Romans 12:20-21.* When our sense of justice is offended, and it is standing in the way of forgiveness, pray. "Lord. I trust in your justice. If my reputation or financial status was harmed by Mr. X, I realize that really it was your reputation and your finances that were harmed, because I am your servant." Trust God to repay.

This is a good place to mention a special circumstance. If your wrongdoer has committed a crime against you or a loved one, by all means notify the authorities. They, not you, serve as an instrument of God's justice on earth. It is the job of the police and the courts to mete out justice. After the arrest, you will want to work on forgiving the perpetrator from your heart, but the Bible does not tell you to let the perpetrator who has committed criminal acts to get off *Scott free*.

In light of the above, try to do something that will bless the wrongdoer! Notice that up until now, you haven't even spoken to the wrongdoer. It has all been between you and God. No. You don't need to go up to the guy and say, "I forgive you." Especially, if he/she hasn't even asked for forgiveness. It has all been between you and God. You have been doing heart work, to mend your own wounded heart. Now it is time to act, not speak. Do something nice to bless the wrongdoer, and don't say a word.

Pray for the wrongdoer. Pray that he/she will see the error of his/her ways and repent, and ask you for forgiveness and reconcile with you. This day may never come. Many times it doesn't, but you should pray for it anyway.

If the time comes that your enemy requests forgiveness, freely give it. If you have followed the above steps, you will be able to forgive your brother or sister from your heart; especially if they have asked for it.

Brothers and sisters. If a person has wronged you, how many times should you forgive them? Not just once or several times, but 7 times 70 times.

As a Christian, you are called to and even mandated to take the love and forgiveness that you have received from God and *pass it on* to those around you. Only then will you be in God's will for your life, and only then will you enjoy the true peace and happiness that passes all understanding!

Bless you all in your walk with Jesus Christ!

Reflections:

FORGIVE US OUR TRESPASSES
AS WE FORGIVE OTHERS

1. Has someone really hurt you in the past? How have you dealt with this injury? Do you still think about it? Have you truly forgiven the person who hurt you? If not, who is hurt worse by your lack of forgiveness, you or the perpetrator?

2. Do you suppose there might be levels of forgiveness? If so, how would you describe them?

3. If you forgive someone, does that mean you must be their friend?

4. Can you forgive someone who is not sorry, and who has not requested your forgiveness? On what levels can you forgive them, and on what levels must you hold back?

5. What are the spiritual consequences of withholding forgiveness? Should we take Jesus seriously when he says that the Father won't forgive us our sins if we don't forgive others?

6. Will uttering the Sinners Prayer be sufficient to receive God's forgiveness, while we continue to hold onto grudges and bitterness? If so, why?

AND LEAD US NOT INTO TEMPTATION
BUT DELIVER US FROM EVIL

*Matthew 4:1 Then was Jesus led up of the spirit into
the wilderness to be tempted of the devil.*
*Matt. 6:13 And lead us not into temptation, but
deliver us from evil...*
*Matthew 26:39 O, my Father. If it be possible, let
this cup pass from me, nevertheless, not as I will,
but as thou wilt.*

In the above three Scriptures, the common theme is temptation.

Specifically, Jesus was either being tempted, or warning us about temptation, or both. In the first scripture, you remember, the Holy Spirit led Jesus out into the desert *in order to be tempted.* As he was out there fasting for 40 days and for 40 nights, the devil came to him and began tempting him with things that he knew Jesus desired.

Jesus was hungry, so the devil asked him to turn rocks into bread. Jesus was contemplating his upcoming mission and his relationship with his Father, so the devil tempted him to *test God* by throwing himself off a rock, to see if angels would really rescue him.

Finally, Jesus knew he had come to establish a Kingdom by first suffering, and Satan tempted him to avoid that suffering, and instead bow before Satan, who would then grant him power and authority over all the kingdoms, without first having to endure the cross. Jesus withstood all of these temptations through his wise use of scripture.

The next scripture is a line from the Lord's Prayer. In His model prayer, Jesus instructs us to pray the following words, *Lead us not into temptation, but deliver us from the evil one.* [NIV]

The last Scripture again shows Jesus at a time of temptation, although it does not explicitly use that word in reference to the Lord. He is in the Garden of Gethsemane right before His trial and crucifixion. He knows what is ahead; Humiliation, rejection, pain, torture and death.

He knows He needs to endure this to accomplish His divine mission, but perhaps He is thinking about those days in the desert when the devil suggested that there is an easier way.

He prays, *Father, if there is a way, take this cup away from me!* But then He overcomes this momentary doubt, and continues, *not my will, but thy will be done.*

It is this moment in the Mel Gibson movie, <u>Passion of the Christ</u> that he stands up and kills the white snake that has been tormenting him with doubts, by stepping on its head.

It is during this time, in the Garden, that He also instructs his disciples to *Watch and pray so that you will not fall into temptation. The spirit is willing, but the flesh is weak." Matthew 26:41* Again, He is instructing them to pray, not to *fall into temptation.*

I remember a famous comedian by the name of Flip Wilson whose trademark slogan was "The devil made me do it!"

He once told a story on the Ed Sullivan Show, which led to his fame. The story was of *The Reverend's Wife and the Dress.*

There once was a reverend, who was married. The wife did not work, and the reverend's salary was quite meager, so they had to live on a tight budget. One day, the wife came home wearing a beautiful brand new dress.

As soon as she walked through the front door, the reverend exclaimed, "What!? Another new dress? That's the third one this week!"

Not to be bullied by her husband, the wife retorted, "I'll have you know, I didn't even WANT to buy this dress. The DEVIL MADE ME buy this dress!"

Surprised, the reverend replied, "That's ridiculous. The Devil didn't MAKE you buy this dress."

The wife held her ground. "How do you know? You weren't even there!"

Knowing he would regret it, the reverend said, "Okay, tell me what happened."

And the wife proceeded to give the following account: "I was just walking down the street, minding my own business, singing one of our choir songs, when suddenly I noticed the devil sneaking up behind me! I turned around and said to myself, *'that's the devil! I'm not even going to acknowledge him!'* But he came up behind me and put his head right up on my shoulder and spoke in my ear and said, 'Hello lady. Look at that beautiful dress in the window. My, you would look good in that dress! Why don't you go in and look at it?' I replied, *'Devil, I don't even want a new dress, and I certainly am not going to go look at it!'* So he starts pushing me right through the door and right up to that dress! Then he says, 'Why don't you try it on? *Try on's* are free, and besides the reverend won't even know!' I said, *'Devil, I am NOT going to try on that dress, I don't even want to buy it!'* But the devil started **threatening me**, until I agreed to try on the dress. Then he said, 'Not only does this dress look REALLY GOOD on you, but it is ON

74

SALE too!' I said, '*Devil, I am not going to buy this dress!*' So the devil took out a gun and made me sign your name on the check to buy this dress!"

When she was finished, the reverend exclaimed, "That is the most ridiculous story I have ever heard! Don't you think it is convenient that the Devil is always MAKING you do things that you want to do anyway? When is the last time the Devil MADE you do something for me?"

Without losing a beat, the wife replied, "Actually the Devil said something about that. He said if it weren't for him, you wouldn't even have a job!"

If you recall the Lord's Prayer, He prays, *Forgive us our debts as we forgive our debtors.*

That line dealt with asking God for forgiveness of past sins and being willing to forgive ourselves what others have done to us.

Now Jesus shifts gears from the past to the present and the future with His prayer. *Lead us not into temptation but deliver us from the evil one.* While the Lord is faithful to forgive our past sins, if we ask Him, He wants us to avoid sinning as much as possible. In order to do this, it is best to steer clear of temptation in the first place.

The Definition of Temptation

The Lord's brother, James, defined temptation as follows: *but each one is tempted when, by his own evil desire, he is dragged away and enticed. Then after desire has conceived, it gives birth to sin; and sin when it is full grown, gives birth to death. James 1:14-15.*

Temptation starts with evil desire.

Contrary to the reverend's wife's assertion that the devil MADE her do things she didn't want to do, have you noticed that you are rarely tempted to do something you are not interested in? If you enjoy gambling, that's the area you are tempted.

We all have our areas where we have evil desires that the devil works on. The devil starts with your own evil desire… like the new dress, despite financial adversity. Unlike the story, though, he does not pull a gun on us. Rather we are enticed.

Notice who does the enticing: In James 1:13 he states, *When tempted, no one should say, 'God is tempting me.' For God cannot be tempted by evil, nor does He tempt anyone.* We are tempted by the Devil and not by God.

Why Does Jesus Ask God Not to Lead Us Into Temptation?

Doesn't James specifically say God does not tempt anyone? Why would Jesus instruct us to ask the Father to *not lead us into temptation?* This is a good question.

We can turn to the Old Testament for guidance. In Proverbs 20:24 the writer states, *A man's steps are directed by the LORD. How then can anyone understand his own way?*

Likewise in Proverbs 16:9, the Word states, *In his heart a man plans his course, but the LORD determines his steps.* If our steps are ordered of the Lord, it makes sense to ask Him to lead us AWAY from temptation.

What I get from the two above proverbs is that God is leading our steps wherever we go! There is a man in our congregation today, who was unable to go on a cruise and is naturally disappointed. I told him, "Praise the Lord! God must have something very important for you to do this week at home." I believe that. He intended to do one thing, but was led on another path by the Lord.

A man's steps are directed by the LORD. If this is true, and we are to avoid temptation, then we should ask the Lord to lead us in a different way. But sometimes, God has other plans.

Sometimes God has His purposes in Leading Us Into Temptation:

This happened to Jesus, when the Holy Spirit led Him into the desert to be tempted by the devil. Matt. 4:1 There, Jesus was tempted by the devil, but He resisted the devil. From this we can determine that temptation in itself is not sin, since the Lord was without sin.

God's purpose was possibly to allow Jesus to be strengthened in his resolve, and to provide an example for us in our struggles with temptation.

You notice the devil used three things that Jesus desired to tempt him, food, assurance that He was God's son, and desire to lead His Kingdom. None of these desires were bad in themselves, but the devil used them as a foothold to try to get Jesus to do things He ought not, to accomplish them. We don't know exactly why, the Holy Spirit led Jesus to be tempted, but we know He did. He had his purpose.

God also allowed Satan to tempt Job, to accomplish His own purpose.

From these Scriptures we can conclude that God sometimes leads us into temptation or allows Satan to tempt us so that we can resist successfully or even fail, in order to achieve a greater good known only to Him.

One example of letting us fail might be where we begin to feel real good about ourselves and our walk with God, and our own personal righteousness, so God gives the devil a little leeway and we fail miserably.

While seemingly a setback if we react properly, and repent, it may lead us to greater acknowledgment of our need for God's grace!

Since God is in control of the entire Universe, it is difficult to conceive of, but sometimes God, while hating evil, allows it to occur in order to achieve a greater good. It is possible, that he even used the *Fall in the Garden of Eden,* in order to allow us to know good from evil, so that when we eventually choose God over sin, we will be more the type of children He desires, than if we had retained our innocence. God is in control.

Temptation Is Something Best Avoided

Apart from God's sovereign purpose in allowing temptation into our lives in order to test or teach us something, *the general rule*, which is stated in the *Lord's Prayer* is that we should pray to *avoid* temptation.

Sin is not good. It is not to be played with or excused. It is harmful and destructive. The wages of sin is death, and therefore, generally, apart from some divine inscrutable purpose, we need to avoid sin at the best of our ability.

Since God directs our steps it is entirely proper to pray to him to LEAD US AWAY FROM,-NOT INTO-TEMPTATION.

We are not strong. Rather than seeking to confront and resist the devil, it is best to stay out of his path. Remember the words of Christ in the Garden of Gethsemane. *The Spirit is willing, but the flesh is weak. Matt. 26:41.* That is why He again directly reminded the apostles there at the Garden, *Watch and pray so that you will not fall into temptation.*

I once heard it said, *We should resolve before we come under temptation that we are going to follow the Lord in a particular area.* This means we are to take precautions to avoid putting ourselves into situations where temptation will take hold of us.

Remember the story of the reverend's wife? She could not avoid glancing at the beautiful dress, but she could have kept walking rather than going into the store to get a closer look, and then trying it on. Now, she could have resisted the impulse to buy the dress at any point. She could have said "no" after entering the store and looking at and picking up the dress. She could have said "no" after trying it on, but her best shot at doing so was when she was still outside. *The Spirit is willing, but the flesh is weak.*

This principle is true for every type of sin!

You teenagers. Do you think it is easier to avoid fornication while you are planning your date, or while you are in the back seat of the car in a lonely place? Don't get into a situation where you are playing with the sin, picking it up and trying it on, then to think that you will have the will power to say "no".

A pastor once told me, you can't always keep a bird from landing on your head, but you can keep it from building a nest. Stop temptation its tracks when it first comes to you, and better yet, stay out of situations where you know you will be tempted.

What are Some Practical Tips for Avoiding Temptation?

Start by praying to God to lead you from temptation. Who knows how many pitfalls you avoid, by just starting here?

Take stock of your desires. The things that motivate you and give you passion. Both good and bad. What are your weak points for sin? What are your strongest points for good? These are the areas where you will be tempted. Think about how you have been tempted in these areas to sin. And take action to avoid these situations beforehand.

I once had a young friend who was in the Vietnamese gangs. He told me, "I don't look for trouble, but trouble always finds me." I told him, "No wonder. You wear gang clothes, and talk gang lingo, and have a propensity to protect your honor and your street rep, and then go to locations frequented by other gang members. It is likely you are going to get into a fight, even though you are not looking for one!"

If your problem is alcohol: Stay away from bars. Don't keep liquor in your house. Avoid friends who drink, and tell others who drink casually of your problem and desire to avoid alcohol. Ask them not to drink in your presence or offer you a drink.

If your problem is pornography. Put filters on your computer, pick an accountability buddy. Don't watch movies that titillate. Don't leer at women all day and think thoughts, and then wonder why you have no discipline to avoid pornography when you're at home alone with the internet.

If your problem is adultery/fornication: Stay away from people you find yourself attracted to. Don't let yourself be alone with them. Don't flirt and then be surprised when they return your affection.

If your problem is gambling/shopping: Don't carry credit cards. Use cash only. Let your spouse keep the cards. Then if you find yourself under a lot of temptation to gamble or shop, you will limit the damage to the cash in your pocket, instead of going into debt with the credit cards.

Finally, figure out what emotions you are feeling right before you fall to temptation. Usually your sin is filling some kind of emotional need. Try to figure out a way to solve the emotional need through your walk with God, rather than engaging in sin.

You must decide beforehand to obey God, and nip your desire in the bud. Remember what James said. It starts with your own evil desire, then you nurture the desire and it turns to sin, and then when sin is full grown it leads to death. The wages of sin is death. Either your own death or death to those around you. Sin has consequences and as Christians, we are dedicated to living for God, and not for the sin that formerly enslaved us.

When we are saved, brothers and sisters, we are not saved from the desire to sin. Instead, we are saved into a lifestyle that understands sin is harmful and hurtful. In our prior lifestyle, we sinned easily and often, as long as we thought we could get away with it.

Now, we understand, that we will never get away with it, so we must resist it. We are saved not into peace, but into a battle with the devil over how we will live our lives. We choose to live for the Lord, but it is not easy to always follow this choice.

Michael L. Faber

But Deliver Us From The Evil One

Many Western Christians and certainly secular people, no longer believe in a personified devil. They believe in God, and the principles of good and evil, but don't really think there is a character named the devil. All I can say is that Jesus believed in the devil, he met him in the desert, and he instructed us to pray to the Lord God to rescue us from the Evil One.

Some of the older translations which rely on newer Greek, read *Deliver us from Evil,* but the oldest Greek manuscripts actually read *Deliver us from the Evil One.*

The record of the Evil One begins in Genesis when the snake told Eve, "You will not surely die, but rather your eyes will be open!" He went on to tempt Job, and Jesus, and Peter warned us about him when he stated, *Your enemy, the devil prowls around like a roaring lion, looking for someone to devour. Resist him, standing firm in the faith because you know that your brothers throughout the world are undergoing the same kind of sufferings. I Peter 5:8.* It is this same devil that John states in the Book of Revelation that will be cast into the Lake of Fire.

We must understand that the Devil is not opposite and equal to God. He is not the Yin to God's Yang. There is an unequal relationship. God created Satan as an angel of light, and Satan used his free will to rebel against God. He has been God's nemesis in God's project to create man, but God has allowed him to operate in order to test our free will to love him and become his people. In the end, God will judge Satan and destroy him.

Satan cannot make us sin. He does not push us in the door or pull a gun on us. But he is crafty and wise. He will use trickery and lies to get us to do what we already want to do. Some will believe his lies so often that they become ensnared and trapped in addiction, sin and death. They are so trapped, that they cannot through their own power ever hope to get out of the mess that they have created. For these people, who are often us, the Lord instructed us to pray, *Deliver us from the Evil One!*

Deliver means to rescue. We need to be rescued from the devil's traps. While we are trapped, Satan will often whisper to us that we deserve what we got, and we can never get away from our particular sin, and instead, that we should just accept it, and maybe even rejoice in our condition, and demand that others accept it as well.

This is true of those struggling in addiction and homosexuality. God does not accept it, and neither should we. We deserve to be free, if we are children of God, because Jesus has already paid the price for our freedom. We need, instead to cry out, LORD RESCUE ME FROM THE DEVIL! DELIVER ME FROM THE EVIL ONE!" If we will do that, He will hear our cry.

Brothers and sisters. No one knows your walk with God. No one can judge it except for the Lord Himself. I have known some who seem to walk on clouds. They have little problem with various sins and seem to accomplish great things spiritually.

Others suffer and struggle with addiction and sin their whole lives. It seems that they never get beyond the devil that has them bound. Victory will come! God does not demand that you achieve victory within a certain time. He merely asks you to have faith, and do your best to resist the devil with the strength He gives you. If you persist in faith, and do not give up, you will prevail!

Whatever you do, never make the final compromise by telling yourself that you cannot overcome your sin, and therefore should just give in. And never let Satan, that great accuser, use your struggles against sin to entice you to give up the faith.

We do not understand God's purposes, but we do understand that we are saved by our faith, not by the results of our works. Yet, simultaneously with this understanding, we know that if we are to call ourselves Christian, we must use everything in our power to resist the devil and his lies.

Hold fast, and never give up! Pray, *Lead us not into temptation* and when things get hard, cry out, *Deliver me from the Evil One!* The Lord will hear that prayer, and He will reach down and save you! Amen.

Reflections

AND LEAD US NOT INTO TEMPTATION, BUT DELIVER US FROM THE EVIL ONE

1. Why might God lead us into temptation? How does praying for him NOT to lead us into temptation affect anything in our walk?

2. What is the best way to avoid sin? How does prayer help in this?

3. Privately, what sins do you struggle with the most?

4. How could you use the suggestions made in this chapter to avoid committing these sins?

5. Why should we bother to avoid sin if we are already saved? What scriptures can you think of that are relevant to this issue?

EPILOGUE

FOR THINE IS THE KINGDOM
THE POWER, AND THE GLORY FOREVER
AMEN

In our worship, we end the Lord's Prayer with the words, *For Thine is the Kingdom, the Power, and the Glory, Forever, Amen*. These words first appeared in the *Didache*, one of the earliest post biblical Christian books, instructing pastors how to *do church*. It was written within decades of the Book of Revelation.

While the words are not in the earliest manuscripts of Matthew or Luke's Gospel, because of Church tradition, the words were later attached at the end of Matthew's Lord's

Prayer in the later Greek Byzantine manuscripts of the Gospel of Matthew, from which the King James Version was translated. If you read from the King James Version you will see them in Matthew 6:13. They do not appear in more recent translations of scripture, but they have been around since the earliest churches met together. Thus, we Protestants have always added these words as part of the Lord's Prayer. In the Eastern Orthodox and Catholic Churches, they are part of the Mass separate from, but just after, the recitation of the Lord's Prayer.

Regardless of the source, and whether Matthew actually penned them, these words have been associated with the end of the Lord's Prayer almost as long as the Bible has been in existence, and they are a fitting end to The Lord's Prayer.

The words, *For Thine* are directed to God. In modern English we could simply say, *Yours*. Everything is God's. He created it all from an overflow of His love. He created the universe from nothing; nothing but His own love. He gave us the Universe, and we declare it is His.

...is the Kingdom... We remember our study above, that our mission is to expand the Kingdom of God, and we are declaring once again, that the Kingdom is *His* and not *Ours*. This is a fact we must well remember, especially if we begin accomplishing things and start to look around at the fruits of our labor. *All of this is Yours, Lord!*

...The Power... All power belongs to God. He can accomplish everything. That is why we pray to Him for our daily bread, for the establishment of His Kingdom, and for protection from evil. It is all within God's power, and we declare this once again by these words.

...And the Glory Forever... Again, we began the Lord's Prayer with a declaration of our desire for God to make His Name holy...because He is a holy, a powerful, and a glorious God...while accessible, loving and full of grace, He is also fearsome...and Other.

Once again, we conclude our prayer, reminding ourselves of the fact that God is indeed glorious, and eternal. What an awesome God we serve!

...Amen... The word Amen does not simply stand for a period at the end of a prayer, but is a statement of faith. It means, *truly, or let it be.* All the things we have said above are true. They always have been true, they are true now, and will be true forever.

Thus ends our walk through the words of the Lord's Prayer. I enjoyed writing this devotional booklet, I hope you enjoyed reading it. May the Holy Spirit give you a blessing for the time you have spent reading these words.

****

JUST A PRAYER AWAY

Perhaps as you have been reading this devotional you have wondered, *Is God really my Father? Am I really His child?* Maybe the thought has cross your mind, *If I were to die today, would I go to heaven? Am I really part of the Kingdom of God right now?* Maybe you feel that there really is very little struggle in your own heart between right and wrong, because you just veer towards the wrong most of the time. These thoughts and doubts may be coming to you for a reason. Maybe you have yet to become a true child of God, truly inheriting that Holy Spirit DNA that will secure a spot for you in God's everlasting kingdom!

Don't despair!

Becoming a true child of God is easy, and it is just one sincere prayer away. The Bible says, *The word is near you; it is in your mouth and in your heart. Romans 10:8.* It goes on to say, *If you confess with your mouth, 'Jesus is Lord', and believe in your heart that God raised him from the dead, you will be saved. For it is with your heart that you believe and are justified, and it is with your mouth that you confess and are saved." Romans 10:9-10.*

Believe in your heart that **Jesus is Lord.** That means that He is both God, part of the Trinity, and Master of your life and destiny. Also, believe that God raised Him from the dead. He, as God, became man, so as to take upon himself the sin of all mankind, including yours. He then allowed Himself to be nailed on a cross to pay the price for your sins and mine. Having paid the price for the sin of all mankind, He declared from the cross, "It is finished." Then He died. But the Father didn't leave Him in that tomb. As a sign that Jesus truly was Lord, and as a sign of heavenly approval, the Father raised the Son from the dead, once and for all conquering the power of death, over sinful man. We are instructed to believe that God raised Him from the dead. By so believing, we acknowledge God's power of life over death, and we acknowledge God's approval of the saving mission of Jesus Christ.

Believing **Jesus is Lord**, is acknowledging His rightful place as Master of our world, and it is submitting oneself to Him as Master of our lives. With this humble attitude, we confess…what do we confess? We confess that we are sinners in need of salvation. We confess that Jesus is willing and able to save us, and we ask for that salvation. The Bible simply says *It is with your mouth that you confess and are saved.* If you would like to join God's forever family, and be a member of the Kingdom of God, living with Him and working for Him for all eternity, you may *enlist* with the following prayer:

LORD JESUS, I HUMBLY DECLARE THAT I AM A SINNER.

I TRY TO DO WHAT'S RIGHT, BUT I'VE FAILED.

I KNOW I CANNOT DO IT ON MY OWN,

I CANNOT MAKE WISE DECISIONS WITHOUT YOUR HELP.

PLEASE, LORD, GUIDE MY LIFE AS LORD AND SAVIOR.

THANK YOU FOR TAKING MY PLACE ON THE CROSS.

I BELIEVE THAT YOU HAVE RISEN FROM THE DEAD

AND YOU ARE SEATED AT THE RIGHT HAND OF THE FATHER.

PLEASE SEND YOUR HOLY SPIRIT TO RESIDE IN MY HEART

AND HELP ME TO BECOME ONE OF YOUR TRUE DISCIPLES.

AMEN

That's it! If you prayed that prayer sincerely, you have commenced a new journey as a child of God! God truly is only a prayer away. But remember, being a child of God does not stop with a single prayer. You are a baby born into God's forever family, but you must be fed, and you must be taught, and you must grow. Your next step is to receive baptism, as an outward sign of the inward miracle that happened today.

Find a group- of godly men and women who are committed to helping you on your faith journey. Finally, read God's word for yourself, and learn as much as you can to successfully fulfill God's will for your life. Remember, after the resurrection of Christ, He declared, *Therefore, go and make disciples of all nations, baptizing them in the name of the Father, and of the Son, and of the Holy Spirit, and teaching them to obey everything I have commanded you. And surely I am with you always, to the very end of the age. Matthew 28:19-20.* He commanded us not just to go out and get people to pray the above prayer, but to baptize them, teach them to be disciples, and obey his commandments. You have signed your enlistment papers today! Now it is time to put on your uniform and learn your orders, and get to work to carry them out!

ABOUT THE AUTHOR: MICHAEL FABER

Michael Faber has been a lay preacher in various Baptist, Presbyterian and Charismatic churches since 1993. He graduated from Fuller Seminary with a Master's Degree in Bible and Theology in 2012, where he learned Greek and Hebrew and the art of textual criticism. He is also a practicing California Attorney.

During his ministry, he has developed a heart for the Vietnamese people. He often preaches at Vietnamese churches (in English) and youth groups. His sermons are often translated contemporaneously by the Vietnamese pastors, so the young people can hear the sermons in English and the older people can hear them in their native language, Vietnamese.

These sermons can be heard online at www.vietchristian.com/sermon or http://www.vietchristian.com/sermon/result.asp?qt=aid&qv=106&fmt=undefined&sort=-3&pid=1

He also serves as a preacher for several retirement homes, offering Sunday services for shut-ins.

Pastor Faber would love to hear from you. You may contact him at mfaber@elkgrove.net.